Major US Historical Wars

The War of 1812

Pamela Toler

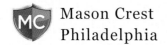
Mason Crest
Philadelphia

Mason Crest
450 Parkway Drive, Suite D
Broomall, PA 19008
www.masoncrest.com

Printed and bound in the United States of America.

CPSIA Compliance Information: Batch #MUW2015. For further information, contact Mason Crest at 1-866-MCP-Book.

3 5 7 9 8 6 4 2

Library of Congress Cataloging-in-Publication Data

ISBN: 978-1-4222-3361-0 (hc)
ISBN: 978-1-4222-8601-2 (ebook)

Major US Historical Wars series ISBN: 978-1-4222-3352-8

About the Author: Pamela D. Toler holds a PhD in history from the University of Chicago. She is interested in the times and places where cultures touch and change each other.

Picture Credits: Everett Historical: 1, 26, 31, 36, 42, 44, 45, 47, 48, 54; Independence National Historical Park, 19, 45 (top right); Library and Archives Canada: 32, 34, 37; Library of Congress: 7, 13, 23, 33, 35, 43 (top center), 46, 51, 52, 56; National Guard Heritage Collection: 29, 49; OTTN Publishing: 11; Joseph Sohm / Shutterstock.com: 53; U.S. Navy History and Heritage Command: 17, 39, 41, 43 (top left; bottom); White House Historical Society: 25.

Table of Contents

KEY ICONS TO LOOK FOR:

Words to Understand: These words with their easy-to-understand definitions will increase the reader's understanding of the text, while building vocabulary skills.

Sidebars: This boxed material within the main text allows readers to build knowledge, gain insights, explore possibilities, and broaden their perspectives by weaving together additional information to provide realistic and holistic perspectives.

Research Projects: Readers are pointed toward areas of further inquiry connected to each chapter. Suggestions are provided for projects that encourage deeper research and analysis.

Text-Dependent Questions: These questions send the reader back to the text for more careful attention to the evidence presented there.

Series Glossary of Key Terms: This back-of-the book glossary contains terminology used throughout this series. Words found here increase the reader's ability to read and comprehend higher-level books and articles in this field.

Other Titles in This Series

Introduction

By Series Consultant
Lt. Col. Jason R. Musteen

Why should middle and high school students read about and study America wars? Does doing so promote militarism or instill misguided patriotism? The United States of America was born at war, and the nation has spent the majority of its existence at war. Our wars have demonstrated both the best and worst of who we are. They have freed millions from oppression and slavery, but they have also been a vehicle for fear, racism, and imperialism. Warfare has shaped the geography of our nation, informed our laws, and it even inspired our national anthem. It has united us and it has divided us.

Valley Forge, the USS *Constitution*, Gettysburg, Wounded Knee, Belleau Wood, Normandy, Midway, Inchon, the A Shau Valley, and Fallujah are all a part of who we are as a nation. Therefore, the study of America at war does not necessarily make students or educators militaristic; rather, it makes them thorough and responsible. To ignore warfare, which has been such a significant part of our history, would not only leave our education incomplete, it would also be negligent.

For those who wish to avoid warfare, or to at least limit its horrors, understanding conflict is a worthwhile, and even necessary, pursuit. The American author John Steinbeck once said, "all war is a symptom of man's failure as a thinking animal." If Steinbeck is right, then we must think. And we must think about war. We must study war with all its attendant horrors and miseries. We must study the heroes and the villains. We must study the root causes of our wars, how we chose to fight them, and what has been achieved or lost through them. The study of America at war is an essential component of being an educated American.

Still, there is something compelling in our military history that makes the study not only necessary, but enjoyable, as well. The desperation that drove Washington's soldiers across the Delaware River at the end of 1776 intensifies an exciting story of American success against all odds. The sailors and Marines who planted the American flag on the rocky peak of Mount Suribachi on Iwo Jima still speak to us of courage and sacrifice. The commitment that led American airmen to the relief of West Berlin in the Cold War inspires us to the service of others. The stories of these men and women are exciting, and they matter. We should study them. Moreover, for all the suffering it brings, war has at times served noble purposes for the United States. Americans can find common pride in the chronicle of the Continental Army's few victories and many defeats in the struggle for independence. We can accept that despite inflicting deep national wounds and lingering division, our Civil War yielded admirable results in the abolition of slavery and eventual national unity. We can celebrate American resolve and character as the nation rallied behind a common cause to free the world from tyranny in World War II. We can do all that without necessarily promoting war.

In this series of books, Mason Crest Publishers offers students a foundation for the study of American wars. Building on the expertise of a team of accomplished authors, the series explores the causes, conduct, and consequences of America's wars. It also presents educators with the means to take their students to a deeper understanding of the material through additional research and project ideas. I commend it to all students and to those who educate them to become responsible, informed Americans.

The text within the cartoon reads:

"I tell you Johnny, you must learn to read Respect — Free trade — Seamans rights &c — As for you Mounfeer Beau Napperty, when John gets his lesson by heart I'll teach you Respect — Retribution &c. &c."

"Ha — ha — Begar me be glad to see Madam Columbia angry with dat dere Bull — But me no learn respect — me no learn retribution — Me be de grand Emperor."

"I don't like that lesson I'll read this pretty lesson"

Chapter 1

Long-Running Disputes Lead to War

I t was May of 1812, and American leaders waited eagerly for the USS *Hornet* to arrive with the latest *dispatches* from England. The *Hornet* had sailed for England in December, only one month after the pro-war faction known as the "War Hawks" had taken their seats in the Twelfth Congress. The ship had carried what one newspaper described as "paper bullets, bloody messages, war resolutions, and frightful speeches." In the months since the *Hornet* sailed, the War Hawks had pushed Congress to the verge of war with Great Britain.

Detail from a political cartoon published around 1813, in which Columbia (an early symbol for the United States, left) chastises both Great Britain (right) and France (center) for their assaults on American rights and interests.

Commercial ties between the two countries had remained strong even after the United States won its independence in the American Revolution. English businesses exported manufactured goods to the former colonies and imported American agricultural products and raw materials. In fact, English merchants sold more goods to the newly independent United States than they had ever sold to the thirteen American colonies. However, America's relationship with Great Britain had grown increasingly strained during the 1790s. Britain had been at war with France since 1793, threatened first by the example of the French Revolution and later by Napoleon Bonaparte's imperial ambitions. Both Britain and France took actions against the rights of ***neutral nations***. U.S. leaders viewed these actions as attacks on its national honor and its economic stability.

Most problematic, from an American point of view, was that new British laws, known as Orders in Council, seemed to be an attempt to push the United States back into the dependence of the colonial period, when America's foreign trade was under British control.

 WORDS TO UNDERSTAND IN THIS CHAPTER

belligerent—a country fighting a war.

blockade—the use of a group of ships to prevent other ships from entering or leaving a port.

contraband—goods that are imported or exported illegally. In time of war, anything that can aid an enemy's army is considered contraband.

dispatch—a message sent from one official to another, often sent by a special method or with great speed.

duty—a tax charged on imports or exports.

economic sanctions—an attempt to force another nation to do something by putting pressure on its economy.

impressment—forced enlistment in the British Royal Navy.

maritime—relating to shipping or navigation.

monopoly—exclusive control.

neutral nation—a country that does not support either side in a war.

By the spring of 1812, the United States was ready to go to war to defend its *maritime* rights and its independence. However, there were rumors that the situation in England had changed. English workers were rioting in Manchester and Birmingham. British factory owners had asked Parliament to repeal the hated Orders in Council that damaged America's trade with Britain. If the rumors were true that England's policy was about to change, there was no reason to go to war. Even the most vehement of the War Hawks was willing to wait for the news.

The *Hornet* docked in New York on May 19. Dispatches from the British Foreign Minister, Lord Castlereagh, reached Washington three days later. Eager to hear the news, people crowded into Secretary of State James Monroe's office. Had England given the United States any reason to back off from the threat of war?

The dispatches were a disappointment. Castlereagh's instructions to the British minister in Washington offered no hope of a change in policy. In fact, he demanded an apology by the United States for its efforts to maintain trade with other European countries.

America's patience had come to an end. On June 1, President James Madison asked Congress for a declaration of war.

Conflicts on the Western Border

The War of 1812 had been brewing for a long time. At the end of the American Revolution in 1783, Benjamin Franklin had warned, "The War of Revolution has been won, but the War of Independence is still to be fought." The Treaty of Paris, which ended the Revolutionary War, had left many problems between the two countries unresolved. Americans still distrusted England. Britons resented the new country that had been formed at their expense, and lost no opportunity to mock the American way of life as uncivilized.

Between 1783 and 1812, the presence of the British colony in Canada on the United States's northern boundary was a constant source of conflict between the two countries. Disputes over the border, the fur trade, and commercial fishing rights were frequent. Most important, American frontiersmen accused the British of supporting Native American uprisings in the Northwest Territory, which consisted of the modern states of

Illinois, Indiana, Michigan, Ohio, and part of Wisconsin.

Conflict over the Northwest Territory was inevitable. The Treaty of Paris had acknowledged that the territory belonged to the United States, but those lands were occupied by Native American tribes that did not feel bound by a treaty that had been signed by their British allies without their agreement. In addition, Britain wanted control over the western fur trade and did not honor its treaty obligations to turn over its posts at Detroit, Michilimackinac, and Niagara. These remained a source of sanctuary and supplies for the Native Americans.

In November and December 1786, a general council of Indians met near Detroit, creating a federation of the Shawnee, Miami, and Kickapoo tribes. The Miami Confederacy agreed that they would only recognize American purchases of Indian lands if all the tribes of the new federation approved them.

The U.S. Congress stated its own claim to the territory in July 1787. The Northwest Ordinance reaffirmed American ownership of the territory and created a process for establishing new states through white settlement. The ordinance claimed that Native American land would not be taken without the Indians' consent except in a "just and lawful" war. However, it did not recognize the authority of the Miami Confederacy to confirm treaties.

Between 1784 and 1786, American commissioners had negotiated treaties for eastern and southern Ohio with small groups of Indians. The Miami Confederacy did not recognize those treaties as legal. Following the passage of the Northwest Ordinance, Congress began selling Ohio land that was still claimed by the tribes of the Miami Confederacy.

Native Americans who saw the Ohio River as the boundary between the American and Indian territories were prepared to fight to defend their right to the land. They were encouraged by British authorities, who thought it was important to maintain their alliance with the Indians. The British also wanted an Indian buffer state that could protect Canada's western boundaries from American encroachment. Indian resistance was answered by raids by the American army against Indian towns along the Ohio, escalating into a major Indian war in the winter of 1789.

Problems in the Old Northwest were solved for a short time after

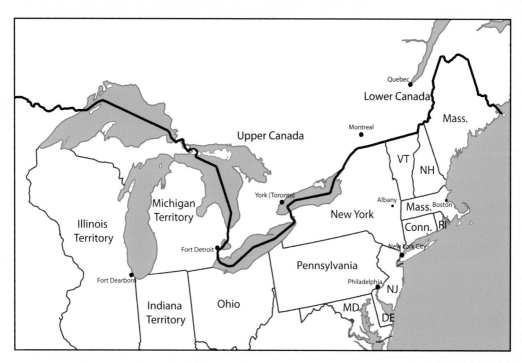

This map shows the Northwest Territory, which bordered the British province of Upper Canada, in 1812. Ohio had been admitted as a U.S. state in 1803, and territorial governments had been established in the remaining lands.

General Anthony Wayne's American army defeated the Miami Confederacy at the Battle of Fallen Timbers in August 1795. The Treaty of Greenville, which was signed after the battle, confirmed the terms of the previously disputed treaties. This gave the United States additional Indian lands in southeast Indiana and southern Ohio, and defined borders between the United States and Indian country.

The British Navigational System

The northern frontier was not the only place where issues left over from America's colonial days created problems between the two countries. Like most European countries of the time, Britain maintained tight control over the economies of its colonies. According to the rules of the British Navigational System, which was designed to give English shipping a ***monopoly*** over trade with British colonies, foreign merchants weren't allowed to trade directly with British colonies. Colonial goods had to be shipped on British ships, or on colonial vessels manned by British sailors.

The American colonies had been an important part of the British colonial economy, both as a market for British goods and as a source of provisions for the British West Indies, as British islands in the Caribbean Sea such as Bermuda, the Bahamas, and Jamaica were known. When the U.S. won its independence, arguments broke out in Britain over whether American ships should be allowed to trade directly with British colonies. British manufacturers and planters in the West Indies wanted America to maintain its former trade relationship with Britain and the colonies. Ship owners wanted to maintain the British Navigational System and keep American ships out.

The shipping interests won, and U.S. ships were only permitted to carry goods to Great Britain itself, not to British colonies in the West Indies or elsewhere. However, merchants in the United States were now free to trade directly with other European countries. As a result, Britain and the United States became commercial rivals as well as trade partners.

Impressment

Life in the British navy was hard and it was difficult to recruit sailors to serve. Instead, Great Britain used "press gangs" to kidnap men from British ports and merchant ships and forcibly enlist them in the British navy. This practice was known as *impressment*.

Impressment became an issue because British seamen regularly deserted their ships and signed on with the American merchant marine, where the pay was better and life was easier. One-fourth of all British sailors abandoned their posts during the French Revolution and Napoleonic Wars. The British Navy claimed the right to stop American ships and search for British deserters.

Legally, only British subjects could be impressed, but in the 1790s and early 1800s it wasn't always easy to tell who was British and who was American. Twenty-five years earlier Americans *had* been British. They still looked and sounded alike. British captains, desperate for sailors, often impressed Americans that they claimed were British subjects. The British government defined an American as someone who had lived in the thirteen colonies prior to 1783, or who was born there. They did not recognize the right of an immigrant to become a citizen of a new country.

A British officer examines seamen on an American ship, looking for deserters from the Royal Navy. The only way for an impressed American sailor to be released was to file a case with the British Admiralty. The Admiralty would order the release of any impressed seaman who could prove he was an American, but this process was difficult and slow.

Between 1793 and 1812, about 6,000 American sailors were forced to serve in the British navy against their will. In 1796, the United States began to provide American sailors with certificates of citizenship to protect them against illegal seizure. However, papers were easy to forge, so even when a certificate was valid, British captains who needed sailors would often ignore it.

Conflicts over Neutral Shipping Rights

The outbreak of war between Britain and France in 1793 brought new tensions to the commercial rivalry between Britain and the United States. As a neutral nation, the U.S. wanted to trade with both Britain and France.

France had a smaller navy than Great Britain and was eager to use ships from neutral countries to import food and supplies. As soon as the war began, France opened its ports to neutral nations and American ships began carrying products from the French West Indies to Europe.

Britain, with the world's most powerful navy, wanted to limit the ability of neutrals to trade with France. It argued that neutral ships could not trade with the French colonies in wartime, because they were not allowed to do so during peacetime. This position was known as the "Rule of 1756." The British had always claimed the right to seize ships carrying ***contraband*** to the enemy; now they expanded the definition of contraband to include food and cloth as well as weapons.

The United States took the position that "free ships make free goods," meaning that a neutral ship could carry anything except contraband with-out being seized by one of the ***belligerents***. The British took the position that "enemy goods make enemy ships." If an American ship was carrying produce from the French West Indies, it was no longer a neutral ship and was therefore subject to seizure. To avoid this, American ship owners used the tactic of "broken voyages"—they would bring a cargo from the French West Indies to an American port and unload it, then re-load it before sail-ing to France so that they could show the cargo as coming from America, rather than a French colony.

During the early years of the European war, these disagreements had little effect on America's trade with either Britain or France. In fact, the European wars provided new opportunities for American trade to flour-ish. Between 1790 and 1802, the number of American ships involved in

 ## THE FRENCH REVOLUTION

The French Revolution began in 1789, when the French nobility tried to limit the power of their king. What began as a power struggle over absolute monarchy led to popular uprisings. In the course of a few months, the monarchy was abolished, the king was imprisoned, and a republic was declared.

In January, 1793, power shifted from reformers to the radical "Jacobins," who executed King Louis XVI and inaugurated the violent period known as "the Terror." Other European powers, including Great Britain, saw the example of the Revolution as a threat to stability at home. When France invaded the Netherlands in February 1793, Britain joined a European coalition against France and went to war.

The French Revolution ended in 1799 when Napoleon Bonaparte seized power. Napoleon (1769–1821) ruled France until 1814, originally as First Consul and later as Emperor. The war between Britain and France ended briefly in 1802 with the Treaty of Amiens, but resumed the next year.

Having crowned himself as emperor in 1804, Bonaparte conquered much of Europe in a series of brilliant military campaigns. The power of the British navy contained his imperial ambitions to the European conti-nent. Napoleon was finally defeated by the British at Waterloo in 1815.

trade to Europe tripled. However, in May of 1803, Napoleon broke the Peace of Amiens and the European war began again. Pressure on American shipping and trade increased almost immediately.

Britain wanted to close loopholes that allowed American ships to provide supplies to France in the name of neutral shipping. The first loophole to be attacked was the fiction of the "broken voyage." The American merchantman *Essex* was seized as a prize of war while transporting cargo from Spain to Cuba, by way of Massachusetts. America protested. The British Admiralty Court reviewed the case and ruled that importing enemy goods into a neutral country did not make those goods neutral unless the ship's captain could prove he had paid an import *duty* on them. In the summer of 1805, the British navy began to seize American ships off the U.S. coast, causing a virtual *blockade* of American ports.

At the same time, arguments over America's trade with the British West Indies renewed in Parliament. The British government proposed a bill that would allow neutral ships to import and export goods to the British West Indies until the war with France ended. Opponents of the bill claimed it was an attack on the British Navigational System. The British colonies could be supplied from Great Britain and Canada, they argued. If supplies from the United States were needed, they could be carried in British ships. In their opinion, American trade with the British Indies would not only damage British shipping and manufacturing, but endanger the security of Britain. The British shipping industry was the primary source of British seamen; anything that affected British shipping damaged Britain's ability to defend itself in the struggle against Napoleon.

War Moves to the Marketplace

By the end of 1805, the war between Great Britain and France had reached a stalemate. The British naval victory at Trafalgar on October 21, 1805, meant that Britain ruled the seas. Following French victories over Russia and Austria at Austerlitz, on December 2, Napoleon effectively ruled Europe on land. As a result, the war between Britain and France developed into a struggle of blockade and counter-blockade, as each side tried to starve the other into surrender. The question of American trade became an important issue for both sides.

In May 1806, the British declared a blockade on the European coast from France to Italy. In response, Napoleon announced the first step in a series of *economic sanctions* against Britain known as the Continental System. The Berlin Decree of November 21, 1806, declared a blockade against England, prohibiting all European trade in British goods. Because he did not have a large enough navy to enforce the blockade at sea, Napoleon created a "reverse blockade." Instead of stopping ships from leaving Britain, he ordered the confiscation of all British goods brought into ports under his control.

The British government responded in January 1807 by extending the Rule of 1756 to outlaw traffic between ports under Napoleon's control. This made it impossible for a neutral ship to drop off a cargo at one European port and pick up a new cargo at another, a common practice that was often needed to make a voyage profitable.

All of these actions were directed at the enemy, but all hurt American trade as well. Events during the next few years would lead the United States and Great Britain closer to conflict.

 TEXT-DEPENDENT QUESTIONS

1. What ship carried a message from the British government to the U.S. government in May 1812?
2. What is the name of the treaty that ended the American Revolution?
3. What modern states were formed out of the lands known as the Northwest Territory?

 RESEARCH PROJECT

Find out about a meatpacker from Troy, New York, named Sam Wilson, who received a contract from the U.S. government to provide food for the U.S. Army during the War of 1812, and how he inspired an iconic American patriotic symbol—Uncle Sam.

Chapter 2

Initial Clashes

By the end of 1803, an increase in the number of impressments led the United States to send diplomats to Britain to protest the seizures from American ships. Britain refused to stop the practice, convinced that their ability to impress sailors was necessary for their battle against Napoleon.

Protests against impressment turned to outrage and calls for war in June of 1807. The commander of the British frigate HMS *Leopard* stopped an American warship, the USS *Chesapeake,* off the Virginia coast and demanded that he be allowed to search the ship for British deserters. When the commodore of the

Chesapeake refused, the *Leopard* fired a shot across the *Chesapeake*'s bow, then launched three **broadsides** at the American ship at close range. Three members of the *Chesapeake*'s crew were killed and eighteen wounded, including the commodore. The British then came aboard and seized four men. Three of them had previously been illegally impressed by the British navy, and had been released after their American citizenship was proven.

Americans screamed for revenge. Rioters in Norfolk destroyed British naval property and state governments called out the **militia**. President Jefferson ordered British warships to leave of American waters. However, he refrained from a declaration of war.

The British government disavowed the *Leopard*'s actions and ordered the Royal Navy to stop waylaying American naval vessels and to be more careful when searching American merchantmen. That wasn't enough to satisfy Jefferson, who demanded the end of impressment of American ships as part of any reparations for the incident. The British refused again.

As a practical matter, the *Chesapeake* incident reduced the illegal impressment of American sailors. However, negotiations regarding British repayment for the damage to the ship and the return of the

 WORDS TO UNDERSTAND IN THIS CHAPTER

ballast—heavy material placed in the hold of a ship to make it more stable on the ocean.

broadside—firing all the guns on one side of a ship at one time.

carrying trade—the business of providing shipping between buyer and seller.

direct trade—the sale of goods directly from seller to buyer.

embargo—a government ban on trade with another country, often including closing ports to ingoing and outgoing ships.

frigate—a high-speed, medium-sized warship used in the nineteenth century.

militia—a military unit composed of citizens who agree to serve for a short term in emergency situations.

impressed sailors continued until 1811, keeping the issue alive in the minds of the American people.

Orders in Council

On November 11, 1807, Britain passed Orders in Council that declared a blockade on every port from which Napoleon excluded British ships. Any ship that entered a port controlled by Napoleon without going to a British port first would be treated as an enemy. The Orders in Council included the right to tax neutral cargos and charge neutral ships for special licenses.

The third president of the United States, Thomas Jefferson (1743–1826) tried to defend America's maritime rights by using economic sanctions against Great Britain and France, rather than force.

Napoleon responded by issuing his own laws, known as the Milan Decrees. They authorized the French Navy to capture any neutral ship that allowed the British to search it, sailed to a British port before going to Europe, or paid British duty on goods.

The British Orders in Council and the Milan Decrees effectively controlled the right of American ships to trade with Europe. Any American ship that tried to bring a cargo into a European port risked being seized, either by the British if the ship had not sailed to England first, or by the French if it had. Between 1807 and 1812, the British and French navies captured almost 900 American ships.

To defend America's maritime rights, President Thomas Jefferson tried to use economic leverage rather than war. Due to their own conflict, Britain and France depended on food and supplies from the United States. Jefferson believed that if the United States refused to ship anything to Europe, Britain and France would be forced to respect America's neutral rights and end impressment of American sailors. In December, 1807, Congress passed the *Embargo* Act, which prohibited exports from the United States from being carried on either American or foreign ships. Foreign goods could be shipped in, but ships leaving American ports could only carry *ballast*.

The people in Britain who were most worried about these economic sanctions were the manufacturers, exporters, and banks involved in the American trade. Their fears were soothed when Napoleon invaded the Iberian Peninsula. Spain and Portugal became British allies and opened their South American and Central American colonies to British trade. This helped to make up for the decline in exports to the United States. In fact, some British merchants claimed that the American embargo helped British trade by keeping American ships out of the newly opened markets to the south.

For his part, Napoleon took advantage of the embargo to order the seizure of American ships in French ports. He argued that these ships must actually be British imposters, since American ships were not allowed to sail to Europe. American merchants lost $10 million dollars worth of ships and cargo.

Ultimately, the embargo was harder on Americans than it was on the British or French. American ships rotted in harbor. Soup kitchens opened in the port cities of New England. Ironically, American sailors, unable to find work at home, took jobs on British ships, lowering the need for impressment. Americans increasingly ignored the embargo, smuggling goods across the Canadian border and disguising illegal cargoes as cobblestone ballast. Harsh enforcement measures created even more anger against the embargo, especially in New England, which was the center of American shipping.

Faced with threats of secession from the New England states, Congress repealed the Embargo Act on March 1, 1809. Three days later, James Madison succeeded Jefferson as president. The embargo was replaced with the Non-Intercourse Act of 1809, which re-opened trade with everyone except Britain, France, and their colonial possessions.

Warfare on the Frontier

In addition to these problems at sea, America faced growing conflict in the Northwest territory.

In the years following the 1795 treaty at Greenville, American settlers poured across the Ohio River to settle the Mississippi River valley. The "permanent" boundaries between American and Indian territories that the treaty had established meant nothing to settlers eager for land.

In 1803, William Henry Harrison, governor of the Indiana Territory, began aggressively negotiating land treaties with neighboring tribes. By 1807, Harrison had negotiated treaties that ceded almost all of Ohio and large portions of southern Indiana, Illinois, Michigan and Wisconsin to the United States. The flood of settlers into those lands inevitably led to renewed Native American resistance, which Americans were quick to blame on British encouragement rather than on American policies.

To a limited extent, American fears were justified. Even after the British finally turned over their Western forts in 1794, British agents continued to provide the tribes with firearms and other supplies. The American outcry following the *Chesapeake-Leopard* incident during the summer of 1807 raised fears that the United States would invade Canada. The Canadian Governor-in-Chief instructed British agents to build stronger alliances with the Indians in case of war without provoking them into premature attacks on the western frontier.

By the beginning of the nineteenth century, 200,000 Americans had settled in Kentucky alone. Isolated farms and individual settlements were in real danger from Indian raids, but as long as the tribes continued to work separately, there was little chance that they could drive American settlers out of the territory altogether.

Around 1805, a Shawnee Indian named Tenskwatawa began to preach a message of religious and cultural revival. Claiming to have seen a vision from the Great Spirit, Tenskwatawa taught that Indians should abandon the ways they had learned from the Europeans and return to their traditional customs. With the aid of the Great Spirit, they could overcome the settlers who were stealing their lands and destroying their way of life. Tenskwatawa became known as the Shawnee Prophet, and his message spread quickly through the Great Lakes region.

Under the leadership of the Prophet's brother Tecumseh, the religious movement became increasingly political. Tecumseh argued that no individual Native American tribe had the right to sell land to Americans, since the land belonged to all of the tribes. Tecumseh wanted to create a federation of Native American tribes that would be strong enough to prevent the movement of American settlers into the western territories. He traveled the Mississippi valley from Ohio to Tennessee, building support among the tribes. Together Tecumseh and his brother successfully united the western tribes against American expansion. Beginning in 1808, increasing numbers of young Indian warriors gathered at the settlement of Prophetstown, located where the Tippecanoe and Wabash Rivers meet.

The British began to encourage the activities of the Prophet and Tecumseh. Americans, meanwhile, blamed the British for Tecumseh's rise to power and for encouraging Indian resistance.

Tensions between Indians and Americans increased after September, 1809, when Governor Harrison signed the Treaty of Fort Wayne with chiefs of the Pottawatomie, Miami, and Delaware tribes. The treaty ceded three million acres to the United States. It angered the members of Tecumseh's federation because the land had been sold without the consent of all the tribes.

In 1810 and 1811, Tecumseh met several times with Harrison to discuss American expansion into Indian lands. Their meetings did nothing to improve relations between Indians and settlers. At their first meeting in the summer of 1810, Tecumseh warned Harrison that no lands in the Northwest could be sold without the approval of all the tribes, and threatened that the chiefs who had signed the treaty would be killed. Their second meeting, in August 1811, began as an armed standoff. Tecumseh arrived with several hundred warriors, while Harrison assembled 800 troops to meet them. Nothing was resolved, though Tecumseh told Harrison that he should not be bothered by the idea of a Native American federation because it was modeled on the example of the United States.

Following their meeting, Indian attacks on outlying American settlements and farms increased. Tecumseh's followers became the focus of American fears regarding another Indian war.

Harrison found himself under pressure to bring peace to the frontier. In November 1811, Tecumseh was away, trying to recruit southern tribes to join his federation. In Tecumseh's absence, Harrison marched toward Prophetstown with a force of 1,000 U.S. soldiers, Indiana militia, and volunteers from Kentucky. On November 7, warriors from Prophetstown attacked the American camp at dawn, expecting the Prophet's special powers to help them overcome the Americans.

American troops charge the Shawnee troops at Prophetstown. Harrison claimed victory at the Battle of Tippecanoe in November 1811, but Native American attacks on the frontier actually increased after the battle.

The Battle of Tippecanoe was no more than a skirmish. About 200 men on each side were wounded or killed. When the Prophet's warriors retreated, Harrison ordered his soldiers to burn Prophetstown to the ground. Although Tippecanoe did little to check the growth of Tecumseh's federation, Harrison claimed a great victory.

In the long run, the cost of the Battle of Tippecanoe to American forces was high. Harrison's expedition convinced many Native American leaders, including Tecumseh, that the American government could not be trusted. This provoked a new round of attacks on American settlements that lasted through the spring of 1812. The Prophet's influence declined because his powers had failed to protect his followers in battle, but Tecumseh continued to recruit Indians to his cause. He would be an important British ally in the early days of the War of 1812.

Sanctions Take Effect

By the spring of 1810, the American government faced opposition on continued economic sanctions against Great Britain from two very different directions. The Federalist party, centered in New England, wanted to come to an agreement with England. At the other extreme, a growing group of western and southern nationalists wanted to go to war.

On May 1, 1810, Congress replaced the unenforceable and unsuccessful Non-Intercourse Act with new legislation known as Macon's Bill #2. It re-opened trade with both Britain and France, and promised that if either of the belligerents revoked the policies that hurt American shipping, the United States would agree to trade exclusively with that country, and stop trading with its enemy.

At first, the British government saw Macon's Bill as a sign that its policy of not making concessions to American concerns had succeeded. Impressment and seizure of neutral ships that violated British blockades were considered essential tools in Britain's struggles against Napoleon. Some British ministers even thought these policies were in America's best interests. The felt that Americans should support England and help it to defeat Napoleon as their best guarantee of continued freedom. Macon's Bill proved that America had come to its senses.

Such British self-congratulation came too soon. In August, Napoleon suggested that he might repeal the Berlin and Milan Decrees. The news reached America in late September, where the vaguely worded assurances were taken as fact, even though France continued to enforce its Continental System policies against neutral ships.

In November of 1810, Madison announced a new trade embargo against British goods and gave Britain three months to repeal its Orders in Council. When Britain took no action, the embargo went into effect on February 2, 1811, with a new twist. British ships and goods were forbidden entry into American ports; American ships and goods were free to go to Britain. Britain could buy, but could not sell.

Madison's threat to restore the embargo against British goods came at a bad time for Great Britain. The closing of Continental markets had created surpluses of British goods that the new South American markets could not absorb. The hard currency on which the economy depended was in short supply because of the long, expensive war with France. And the newly opened markets of South America had not proved as profitable as British industries had expected.

Industrial England plunged into an economic depression caused by the loss of both American markets and American raw materials. Without American cotton, textile factories were forced to close. Manufacturers of pottery and hardware shut down because they could not sell their products. Unemployed factory workers rioted, attacking the machines that they thought were the cause of their poverty. British troops were required to keep the peace.

In May 1811 Parliament began to receive petitions from the manufacturing districts of Britain calling for the repeal of the November, 1807, Orders in Council. Manufacturers testified that trade with the United States was vital to the British economy, and blamed the government's policies for the economic depression.

James Madison (1751–1836) served as Secretary of State under Thomas Jefferson and succeeded him as president in 1809. Madison shared Jefferson's preference for a peaceful solution to the U.S. dispute with Great Britain, but was pressured into asking Congress to declare war.

A Divided Nation

The United States was divided in two different ways: between the settled areas in the east and the western frontier and between the commercial states of the north and the planter states of the south. The Napoleonic Wars affected different areas of the United States in different ways.

In the early years of the Napoleonic Wars, New England enjoyed a shipping boom from the wartime ***carrying trade***. Even after the system of blockades was put in place, New England ships continued to sail; if only one ship in three was able to deliver its cargo the ship owner could still make a profit. Prices for corn, beef, and flour rose as the farms of the mid-Atlantic states fed General Wellington's army in Spain.

The planters of the south and the frontiersmen of the west were not directly affected by limitations on the carrying trade or the impressment of seamen, but they were still hurt by the blockades and counter-blockades of the Napoleonic Wars, which closed the overseas market for their

As leader of the pro-war faction known as the "War Hawks," Henry Clay (1777–1852) pressured President Madison and Congress into declaring war on Great Britain; he would later serve on the team that negotiated peace in 1814. Clay continued to serve in the House of Representatives until his death in 1852 and ran unsuccessfully for President four times.

farm produce. As the prices of cotton, hemp, and tobacco dropped, southern planters and western farmers came to believe Britain's economic policies were the source of all their troubles.

Caught in the throes of an agricultural depression, the south and the Mississippi Valley enthusiastically supported measures designed to force the European powers to repeal the restrictions on American trade. When economic sanctions failed, they clamored for war.

War Hawks

A new group of men took their seats in Congress in November 1811, three days before the Battle of Tippecanoe. Disgruntled voters had replaced sixty-three of the 142 members of the House of Representatives. The new men were eager to fight the British, driven by the desire for continued expansion to the west, fear of British-backed Indian resistance, the loss of foreign markets, and concern over the falling prices for farm products. The so-called "War Hawks" were mostly from the West and the South. Their leaders included John S. Calhoun of South Carolina, Henry Clay of Kentucky, and Felix Grundy of Tennessee. Clay was elected Speaker of the House on his first day in office. He used his power to make committee appointments to pack important committees with fellow War Hawks. Although they did not have a majority of the votes, the War Hawks soon found themselves in control of the Twelfth Congress.

Of the 142 members in the House of Representatives, only ten were from the frontier states of Kentucky, Ohio, and Tennessee. (The territories of Indiana, Illinois and Michigan were not yet states and did not have representation in Congress.) Even taking into account the less-settled areas of the coastal states, it was impossible for the West to drag the United States into war alone. The War Hawks had to persuade the other members of Congress that war was necessary.

The War Hawks argued for war from November 1811 to June 1812. Taking the motto "Free trade and sailors rights," they cited the Orders in Council, illegal blockades, impressment, neutral rights, and national honor as reasons for going to war. They took the position that the issue was not the carrying trade, but the ***direct trade***, what Clay described as "the right to export our cotton, tobacco and other domestic produce to market." They argued for the conquest of Canada as the best way to wage war against an enemy they could not hope to defeat at sea. In only four months, they passed the laws needed to prepare for war, putting the legal machinery in place to increase the size of the army, call out the state militias, purchase weapons, build coastal fortifications and borrow money.

In April of 1812, Congress passed a 90-day embargo against British goods and shipping as a first step toward declaring war while they waited for the USS *Hornet* to return with the latest dispatches from Europe.

The *Hornet* reached New York on May 19. Three days later, dispatches from the British Foreign Secretary, Lord Castlereagh, arrived in Washington. Unofficial sources had reported that British policy was on the verge of changing, but Castlereagh's dispatches did not confirm this rumor.

However, unknown to the Americans, Castlereagh's dispatches no longer reflected Parliament's position on the Orders in Council. On May 11, Prime Minister Spenser Percival, the most stubborn supporter of the Orders in Council, had been shot to death over a personal matter. Without a leader, the Tory government was forced to resign. Presented with a growing number of petitions against the Orders in Council and proof of the damage they were causing the British economy, the interim leaders of Parliament moved toward repealing the Orders.

President James Madison had no way of knowing about this. On June 1, Madison sent a message to Congress asking for a declaration of war against Great Britain. His message argued that Britain was already fighting an undeclared war against the United States by its actions to restrict American free trade and the alleged incitement to violence of Indian tribes. On June 11, the U.S. House of Representatives voted 74 to 49 in favor of war. After five days of ferocious debate, on June 18 the U.S. Senate passed the measure by a vote of 19 to 13.

The British Parliament revoked the Orders in Council on June 16, 1812, two days before the United States Senate voted to go to war. News of the repeal didn't reach Washington until after the fighting had begun.

If Parliament had made this decision even a month sooner, it is possible the war would not have occurred. Madison later claimed that if he had received the news earlier, he would not have called for war.

The road to the War of 1812 was paved with misunderstandings and bad timing. Despite their shared past, America and Britain viewed events that occurred between 1793 and 1812 in totally different ways. Americans saw every British decision as an attack on America's fragile economic freedom. The British made the mistake of assuming that the United States would see Britain as the lone defender of liberty against Napoleonic tyranny.

 ## TEXT-DEPENDENT QUESTIONS

1. What 1809 treaty angered members of Tecumseh's federation? Why?
2. Why did British factory owners want to resume trade with the United States in 1809?
3. What British prime minister was the strongest supporter of the 1807 Orders in Council?

 ## RESEARCH PROJECT

Using the Internet or your school library, learn more about the members of Congress who were leaders of the "War Hawks" faction that wanted the United States to declare war on Great Britain in 1812. Choose one of the War Hawks, and write a two-page report about his political career and accomplishments. Share your report with the class.

Chapter 3

The Struggle for Canada

When the War of 1812 began, Americans expected to easily conquer Canada. The British colony was defended by only 6,000 British soldiers. Even former president Thomas Jefferson, who had tried so hard to maintain the peace during his term, thought that the American capture and annexation of Canada would be "a mere matter of marching." British leaders had the same concerns.

The Unites States was not prepared for war, however. Five years of self-

Members of a Kentucky militia ride into battle against British soldiers. The U.S. Army was very small when the War of 1812 began, so state militia units were expected to take part in offensive actions such as a proposed invasion of Canada.

imposed commercial isolation had weakened the economy. In addition, after the Revolutionary War Americans had been afraid of the idea of maintaining a large army. In June 1812 the entire U.S. Army only contained about 11,000 trained soldiers. Many senior officers were elderly veterans of the American Revolution, fought 30 years earlier. A few younger officers had seen combat against Native Americans, but had never fought a European-style war, especially not against one of the best military forces in the world.

In 1811 Congress had authorized that the U.S. Army be expanded to 35,000 men. It would take time to recruit and train the additional soldiers, however, so in the meantime American leaders expected state militias to take part in the fighting. Militias were often called upon to defend their states from Native American attacks, and during the Revolution they had at times played an important role in the fight for American independence. However, state militias were often poorly equipped and untrained. Some states, such as those in New England, refused to send their militias to the war.

One advantage that the United States had going into war was that Great Britain was focused on the war against Napoleon in Europe. Though Anglo-American affairs were all-important in the United States, in England they were at most a distraction compared to Britain's struggle for survival against France.

A Disastrous Invasion

In May 1812, before war was declared, Madison had appointed General William Hull to lead a military force to Fort Detroit, on the Canadian border. Hull had been a decorated officer during the American Revolution.

 WORDS TO UNDERSTAND IN THIS CHAPTER

artillery—heavy guns, including cannons and mortars.
garrison—a body of troops stationed at a fortified place such as a fort.

However, in 1812 he was nearly 60 years old and had not been involved with the military in many years. Hull's force consisted of about 300 U.S. Army soldiers, supplemented by 1,200 militiamen. He arrived on the U.S.-Canada border in early July. Once he received word that the war had begun, Hull brought his men across the Detroit River to begin the invasion of Canada.

Hull was fearful that the Shawnee and other Native American tribes would ally themselves with the British and overwhelm his small force. He wrote to Washington requesting reinforcements, and also asked for a naval fleet on Lake Erie that would help protect Detroit and other American forts along the cost. His requests were ignored by the Secretary of War, William Eustis. Hull's small army was also short of food, a reflection of the poor state of preparation by the U.S. government before the war began. To

When William Hull's army landed in Canada, the general issued a boastful proclamation of his intent to conquer the territory. "I come prepared for any contingency," Hull wrote. "I have a force which will break down all opposition, and that force is but the vanguard of a much greater." Hull's rhetoric could not quite match his actions in Canada, however.

feed his men, he had to confiscate supplies from Canadian farmers, an action that did not endear the Americans to the Canadians.

On the British side, the territorial governor Isaac Brock took charge of the defense. Brock had been preparing for the prospect of war, and his militiamen were trained and ready to fight. He had also contacted Tecumseh and other Native American leaders, asking them to fight on the British side if Canada was invaded. Tecumseh, who distrusted the

Fort Mackinac held a small number of American soldiers. When a British force arrived to demand that the fort surrender, American commander Porter Hanks was not even aware that war had been declared. The incompetent U.S. Secretary of War William Eustis had sent the news by the regular postal service, which could take weeks to arrive, rather than by a special messenger.

Americans due to Tippecanoe, pledged that the Shawnee would side with the British. He soon convinced other tribes to do the same, and about 600 Native American warriors joined the 700-man British force.

Hull began to worry when the British captured a small American outpost on Mackinac Island, capturing 75 men without a shot being fired. After a Native American war party surprised a group of 200 American soldiers, killing half of them, Hull began to panic. He soon ordered his men to withdraw back across the border to Fort Detroit. Hull was so obviously scared that the officers and men under his command soon began asking for him to be removed as their leader.

Brock's British soldiers and their Indian allies beseiged the Americans at Fort Detroit. Hull was unable to get food and supplies in Fort Detroit, because British ships controlled Lake Erie. Although Brock's men were outnumbered, they bluffed the Americans into thinking their force was much larger. At night the British lit numerous extra cooking fires, and during the day they would allow the Americans to see their units marching from place. The men would then duck down behind defenses, move to another area, and march again. These strategies helped create the illusion that the British and Indian force was two or three times as large as it really was.

On August 16, 1812, as Brock's army approached Fort Detroit, they were met by an officer carrying a white flag. Hull surrendered the fort without a fight, turning over about 3,000 muskets, 37 cannons, and 100,000 musket cartridges to the British. The surrender was viewed as a major disgrace for the U.S. military.

Hull later claimed that he surrendered Detroit without a fight in part because he was afraid that a battle would result in hundreds of women and children at the fort being massacred by the Indians. This happened at another American outpost, Fort Dearborn, located on Lake Michigan in the Illinois Territory. While still in Fort Detroit, Hull had ordered that Fort Dearborn be evacuated, as he did not believe it could be defended. The small American *garrison*—54 soldiers, 12 militia, nine women, and

This political cartoon, published in the fall of 1812, denounces the "humane" British and their Indian allies. The officer's comment, "Bring me the Scalps and the King our master will reward you," refers to Colonel Henry Proctor's policy of paying Native Americans for scalps taken from American soldiers. This was a common practice among Indian warriors that occurred throughout the war. Americans committed their own atrocities, burning Indian villages and killing Native American women and children at times.

18 children—were trying to reach Fort Wayne in the Indiana Territory when they were attacked on August 15 by warriors of the Potowatomie tribe. Half of the soldiers and all of the militia were slaughtered, along with two women and 12 children. The rest were taken prisoner.

Continued U.S. Failures in Canada

After this disappointing start to the war, American officials wanted to establish a foothold in Upper Canada before the winter set in, making military campaigns impossible. A force of about 6,000 soldiers and militia under General Stephen Van Rensselaer was sent to cross the Niagara River and capture Queenstown.

Again, the choice of American commander proved to be a poor one. Rensselaer was a politician, not a soldier, and had never commanded troops in battle. Some of the regular army officers refused to follow, or even acknowledge, his orders. In the meantime, Isaac Brock learned of the threat and came to Queenstown to supervise the town's defense.

Isaac Brock (1769–1812) became known as the "Hero of Upper Canada" for his successful defense of the region from invading American troops in 1812. He was mortally wounded while leading his men to victory at Queenstown Heights.

On October 13, 1812, about 3,000 Americans crossed the Niagara River and assaulted Queenstown. The British had posted their **artillery** on a high bluff that overlooked the river, and cannon fire pinned down the Americans when they landed. The Americans assaulted the heights, capturing the British artillery and killing some of the defenders, including Brock. However, with victory still possible members of the New York militia retreated across the river, and refused to rejoin the battle. British reinforcements arrived from Fort George, and the remnants of the American invasion force on Canadian soil surrendered.

The loss of General Brock was a serious blow to the defense of Canada. Nonetheless, the Canadians were encouraged by their unexpected victories, as many had not believed they could resist an American invasion. They also inspired many Native American tribes to join the British in the fight against the Americans. On the American side, leaders were beginning to realize that they would not win an easy victory in Canada. Two other military offensives that had been proposed for 1812—one intended to gain control of Lake Champlain and Montreal, and the other to seize the St. Lawrence River—were soon cancelled.

Defense of Fort Wayne

With the loss of the American forts at Detroit, Mackinac, and Dearborn, the entire frontier west of Ohio fell under British control, and the American settlements in the Indiana Territory were open to attack. The main American fort in this area was Fort Wayne, which had a small garrison of about 100 soldiers. It had once been a strong outpost, with walls strong enough to withstand cannon fire, but the fort had become run down in the early 1800s.

William Henry Harrison described the Shawnee war leader Tecumseh (1768–1813) as "one of those uncommon geniuses, which spring up occasionally to produce revolutions and overturn the established order of things." Tecumseh fought as a British ally in the War of 1812 until his death at the Battle of the Thames in October 1813.

The commander at Fort Wayne, Captain James Rhea, learned about the loss of Fort Dearborn from survivors of the massacre who reached the outpost on August 26. American patrols soon indicated that Native American warriors were arriving in the area of the fort, and on August 28 a local fur trader was killed near Fort Wayne.

In September of 1812, large numbers of warriors from the Potawatomi and Miami tribes began to gather around Fort Wayne. They were led by Potawatomi Chief Winamac, who had fought against the Americans at Tippecanoe, and Chief Five Medals. The two chiefs met with Captain Rhea

As governor of the Indiana territory from 1800 to 1811, William Henry Harrison (1773–1841) negotiated land treaties with Indian tribes in the Old Northwest that increased Indian resistance to white settlement. In November 1811, he led a campaign against Tecumseh and the Shawnee Prophet that ended at the Battle of Tippecanoe. Harrison later became the ninth president of the United States, but died of pneumonia just a month after his inauguration.

on September 4. They told him that other frontier forts had already been captured, and said that Fort Wayne would be the next to fall. Over the next week, the Americans repulsed many attacks.

Relief arrived in the form of General William Henry Harrison, leading 2,200 member of the Kentucky militia. On the way, Harrison's small army was joined by 800 militiamen from Ohio. With Harrison's troops approaching, Winamac launched a final attack against Fort Wayne on September 11. It failed, and the Native Americans withdrew before Harrison's force reached Fort Wayne.

A New American Offensive

When he arrived at Fort Wayne, Harrison immediately took charge of the fort. For several weeks he used it as a base from which to attack neighboring Indian villages, reducing attacks on the American settlements. The government soon appointed Harrison a general in the regular army, and he spent some time training a large number of new U.S. Army recruits that arrived at the fort.

The strategic plan for the U.S. military involved the recapture of Detroit, and Harrison was chosen to lead this campaign. It was unusual for military campaigns to be waged during the winter months, but the American public demanded action. In late October of 1812, Harrison started north toward Lake Erie with an army of about 6,500 men. He divided his force, sending about 1,000 men under the command of General James Winchester toward Frenchtown, a settlement on the Raisin River in the Michigan Territory that had been occupied by the British after the fall of Fort Detroit.

In January of 1813, fighting in deep snow, Winchester's small army drove the British, Canadian militia, and about 200 of their Native American allies out of Frenchtown. However, Winchester did not fortify the town, and was unprepared when a larger force of 600 British regulars and 800 Native Americans attacked on January 22. Most of the American army was quickly killed or captured; Winchester was seized by Indians and handed over to the British commander, Colonel Henry Proctor.

About 400 riflemen from Kentucky had continued to fight from behind a split-log fence. Proctor demanded that the captive Winchester order these men to surrender. The Kentucky militiamen initially refused, but after three more hours of fighting and British promises of safety and good treatment for the wounded, they laid down their weapons.

The British promises would not be kept. Proctor was worried that Harrison's larger force might arrive at any time, so the British soldiers soon left the battlefield. They took some of the American prisoners with them, but many of the wounded Americans were left behind. On January 23, the restive Native Americans, angry at their own losses in the battle, began to plunder the wounded men. They set fire to the cabins where the men were sheltered, and scalped and killed those who tried to escape. Roughly 100 Americans were killed in what became known as the Raisin River Massacre.

This painting shows American troops crossing the frozen Raisin River to capture the town of Frenchtown in January 1813.

American plans for revenge had to be postponed, as Harrison decided to suspend military operations for the winter. He built two forts in Ohio, Fort Meigs and Fort Stephenson, and posted his army near the Michigan border at the western end of Lake Erie. Harrison told American leaders the same thing that William Hull had—that a naval force was needed to gain control of the Great Lakes so that the army's 1813 campaign into Canada could succeed. By this time, American government leaders were willing to listen.

TEXT-DEPENDENT QUESTIONS

1. What size U.S. Army did Congress authorize in 2011?
2. How did the British and their Native American allies bluff General William Hull into thinking their force was larger than it really was?
3. What American general led a force of 3,000 men to relieve Fort Wayne from a siege by Native Americans?

RESEARCH PROJECT

The musket was the primary weapon of most infantry soldiers during the War of 1812. Do some research on this type of firearm. What was the range, and how accurate were these weapons? Were there any limitations or drawbacks to using them? Write a one-page report on what you learn.

Chapter 4

Victories at Sea and on Land

When the War of 1812 began, most people believed the best opportunity for a U.S. victory lay in gaining control of Canada through a land war. Britain's Royal Navy was considered too powerful for America to attack; indeed, it was the most powerful naval force in the world. In 1812 the Royal Navy included 219 of the largest warships, known as ships of the line, each armed with 74 cannons or more. The British also had 296 fast and maneuverable warships, known as frigates, each armed with around 38 to 44 guns, as well as

Just a few weeks after the War of 1812 began, USS Constitution *proved that American ships could defeat powerful warships of the Royal Navy when it outfought the British frigate HMS* Guerriere *off the Canadian coast.*

hundreds of smaller ships. By contrast the U.S. Navy had just twenty ships, only nine of which were frigates.

However, in the early years of the War of 1812, America's successes mostly came in naval engagements. The first of these was one of the most famous battles in American history, when the American frigate USS *Constitution* defeated a British frigate, HMS *Guerriere*, on August 19, 1812. *Constitution* was commanded by Isaac Hull, a nephew of the American general who had surrendered Fort Detroit to the British a few weeks earlier. The 44-gun frigate, one of the largest American ships, was sailing from Boston, looking to raid British merchant ships off the coast of Canada. It encountered the British warship about 400 miles southeast of Halifax, Nova Scotia.

The *Constitution* had the advantage of a wooden hull that was thicker than *Guerriere*'s. Early in the battle, a shot fired from *Guerriere* bounced harmlessly off the *Constitution*, leading one of her sailors to shout, "Hurray! Her sides are made of iron!" This would lead to the American warship's famous nickname, "Old Ironsides." As the warships got closer, the *Constitution*'s heavier guns pounded the *Guerriere*. The ships drew close enough for the American and British marines on board each vessel to fire their muskets at the enemy, causing casualties on both sides. After about 20 minutes, *Constitution*'s gunners knocking down the *Guerriere*'s masts and disabled the ship. Unable to maneuver or fire back, the British captain surrendered.

Captain Hull wanted to tow the *Guerriere* back to the United States, but it was too badly damaged and was sinking. He brought more than 200 British sailors aboard the *Constitution* and returned to Boston. Hull

 WORDS TO UNDERSTAND IN THIS CHAPTER

privateer—a private ship licensed by the government to raid enemy ships in times of war.

territorial waters—Inland and coastal waters under a country's control, usually ocean waters within three miles of the coastline.

In naval battles during the War of 1812, ships would try to knock down the masts and rigging of enemy ships in order to disable them. This painting shows the U.S. frigate Constitution *having demasted the* Java *during the December 1812 encounter.*

arrived in port ten days later, and the news soon spread that a U.S. Navy ship had defeated a British warship in combat. News of this victory provided a huge boost to American morale, which had fallen with the loss of Fort Detroit.

Another notable American victory occurred in October 1812, when the frigate USS *United States*, commanded by Stephen Decatur, captured HMS *Macedonian* after a battle. Decatur was able to prevent the ship from sinking, and brought it back to Newport, Rhode Island. *Macedonian* was repaired and became part of the U.S. naval fleet.

A few weeks later, *Constitution* set out again under a new commander, William Bainbridge, sailing south to the British sea lanes near Brazil. On December 29 the ship encountered HMS *Java*, a British frigate about the same size as *Guerrière*. Once again, after an intense battle *Constitution* disabled the British warship and forced it to surrender.

The success of the American frigates was supplemented by thousands of small encounters fought by American ***privateers***, who waged war by

The Royal Navy won their share of victories during the War of 1812. This painting shows the British frigate Shannon *capturing the USS* Chesapeake—*the same unlucky ship that had been fired on by the British in 1807—during a battle off the coast of Massachusetts in May 1813.*

capturing British merchant ships. Privateers were privately owned ships whose captains or owners would receive a license, called a letter of marquee, from the U.S. government to attack enemy ships. The owners would arm their ship with one or more cannons, and if they encountered an enemy ship they would try to force it to surrender. Privateers had to be daring in order to capture another ship. Often, a privateer might only have a few guns at first, but once they captured a ship they would take its cannons and add them to their arsenal.

During the War of 1812, American privateers captured about 1,350 British merchantmen, worth more than $40 million. They sank many other ships, devastating Britain's commercial shipping. Within a few years, British insurance companies were charging high rates to British shipowners because of the danger from American privateers.

The Attack on Canada Resumes

In late 1812, Secretary of War William Eustis resigned, and in January 1813 General John Armstrong was appointed to the position. Armstrong

American officers had an important impact on the war during 1813, including (left to right) naval hero Oliver Hazard Perry (1785–1819); Winfield Scott (1786–1866), who would become the foremost American military commander during the first half of the 19th century; and Zebulon Pike (1779–1813), who had gained fame as an American explorer before the war.

was a veteran of the American Revolution, and he understood that control of the Great Lakes was necessary for a successful invasion of Canada. He developed a plan to attack the Royal Navy's base at Kingston early in 1813, before the St. Lawrence river thawed and British reinforcements could arrive. The plan initially involved a joint attack by 7,000 U.S. Army soldiers, led by General Henry Dearborn, and a naval assault by a small fleet commanded by Commodore Isaac Chauncey. Both of these forces were based near Sackett's Harbor, New York, where there was an American shipyard. However, the plan was soon changed to an attack on York (now known as Toronto), the capital of Upper Canada, which was not as well defended as Kingston.

On April 26, 1813, Chauncey's fleet of 14 ships bombarded the British fort at York while about 2,000 American soldiers landed near the city. They were led by General Zebulon Pike, an experienced officer, and quickly routed the British defenders. However, as they retreated the British blew up an ammunition storage building, which killed many Americans, including Pike. The British also destroyed a warship

Isaac Chauncey (1779–1840) was responsible for the successful U.S. naval strategy on the Great Lakes in 1813.

During the Battle of Lake Erie, the British squadron consisted of six ships with 63 cannons, most of which could fire at longer range than the American ships. Perry's squadron of nine vessels was armed with a total of 54 guns.

so that it would not fall into American hands. In anger about these developments, American soldiers looted and burned York.

The Americans did capture a number of cannons and other military supplies. These were sent to Presque Isle, in Lake Erie off the coast of Pennsylvania, where navy shipbuilders commanded by Lieutenant Oliver Hazard Perry were working on another American fleet for the Great Lakes.

After the victory at York, Chauncey's fleet transported the American soldiers to Fort Niagara, across the lake, where they prepared for an assault on another British stronghold, Fort George. The Americans launched that attack early in the morning of May 27. Perry, who had come to Fort Niagara looking for sailors, was in charge of gunboats that bombarded Fort George, while American troops landed and assaulted the fort. An American unit under Colonel Winfield Scott successfully captured the fort, which the Americans would hold for the rest of the year. The victory gave the U.S. military control over Lake Ontario.

U.S. troops might have exploited this victory by chasing the retreating British army, but they delayed. In the meantime, the movement of troops and Chauncey's squadron had left Sackett's Harbor lightly defended. On May 29, British troops were transported across Lake Ontario and attacked the town. The Americans suffered many casualties, but drove them away.

Victory on Lake Erie

By the late summer of 1812, Oliver Hazard Perry's Lake Erie fleet was complete. Although his ships were manned with inexperienced sailors, Perry was ready for a fight. The British naval commander on Lake Erie, Commander Robert Barclay, commanded six ships, including HMS *Detroit*, which carried 20 guns, and the 16-gun *Queen Charlotte*. Perry's fleet of nine ships included his flagship, the USS *Lawrence*, and the USS *Niagara*, both of which had just been constructed at Presque Isle and carried 20 guns. The battle between the two squadrons on September 10, 1813, was the first full-fledged clash between the British and American navies; previous battles had involved single ships from each country.

When the battle began, Perry moved the *Lawrence* forward. The *Niagara* held back from the battle while *Lawrence* took a pounding from the British ships. After two hours, every gun on the *Lawrence* had been destroyed, and most of Perry's men were dead. The commander lowered

Commodore Perry transfers his battle flag from the damaged Lawrence *to the* Niagara *under fire during the Battle of Lake Erie. This was a dangerous maneuver, as the British attempted to sink Perry's small boat.*

This 19th century drawing of the Battle of the Thames depicts Colonel Richard Johnson shooting the Shawnee leader Tecumseh. Johnson led the Kentucky militia in a charge that routed the British and Native Americans. Although he later claimed to have killed Tecumseh, no one knows who fired the fatal shots at the Native American leader.

his flag, which included his motto "Don't Give Up the Ship." In a small boat, he was rowed to the *Niagara*, where he took command and brought that ship into the battle. The British ships had been badly damaged, and the *Niagara* succeeded in firing broadsides into *Detroit* and *Queen Charlotte*. After another hour of fighting, Commander Barclay, who was badly wounded during the fighting, surrendered.

The victory on Lake Erie enabled an American army under General Harrison to capture the Canadian town at Amherstburg, as well as to recapture Fort Detroit without a fight on September 27. The British army retreated up the Thames River.

William Henry Harrison left about one-third of his soldiers at Amherstburg and Detroit, and led the rest in pursuit of the retreating British army commanded by Henry Proctor. Tecumseh had protested leaving without a fight, but the Native Americans had no choice but to join the British retreat.

Harrison's army of about 3,700 men, most of whom were militia from Kentucky, caught up with the British and Indians on October 5, near the settlement of Moraviantown on the Thames River. Proctor commanded a force of about 800 British soldiers and 500 Native Americans. The Battle of the Thames lasted less than an hour, with American militiamen charging into the fray shouting their battle cry, "Remember the Raisin!" The Americans lost only 24 men, while inflicting significant casualties on the

British and Native Americans. Most damaging, however, was the death of Tecumseh during the battle. He had united many Native American tribes against the United States, but without his leadership the coalition he tried to build would soon fall apart.

The Creek Wars

To the south, in the Mississippi Territory, a powerful native American tribe known as the Creeks were experiencing a civil war. The Creeks had historically been friendly to the United States, but some younger warriors of the tribe, encouraged by Tecumseh, had decided to fight against the Americans. Members of this faction painted their war clubs bright red; they became known as the Red Sticks.

A skirmish against American militia occurred in July 1813 at Burnt Corn Creek. A month later, a band of Red Sticks overran Fort Mims in the Mississippi Territory (in present-day Alabama), and slaughtered more than 500 Americans and friendly Creeks that were taking shelter there.

With U.S. troops engaged in Canada, the defense against the Creeks was entrusted to state militias from Georgia and Tennessee, as well as from the Mississippi Territory. General Andrew Jackson was placed in charge of the militia campaign against the Creeks. Over the next several months, Jackson's militia defended American settlements in the territory

The Fort Mims massacre occurred in part because the commander of the American garrison did not take precautions. One of the fort's gates was left open when the Red Sticks arrived. The warriors burst into the fort, killed nearly everyone inside, and then set it on fire. It was the first time that Native Americans had overwhelmed an American fort without British help.

The Red Sticks nicknamed Andrew Jackson (1767–1845) "Sharp Knife" due to his tenacity and aggressive attacks on the battlefield.

and sought out hostile Creek warriors. Jackson formed an alliance with the Cherokee tribe, who traditionally were enemies of the Creeks. A small faction of Creeks also remained friendly with the United States and opposed the Red Sticks.

In March 1814, American and Creek forces met at Horseshoe Bend in Alabama. The Red Sticks had built strong defenses, but Jackson had about three times as many soldiers, and he was able to overwhelm the Native Americans. More than 800 of the Creek warriors were killed, compared to just 47 American soldiers.

The Battle of Horseshoe Bend marked the end of Creek fighting during the War of 1812. After the battle, Jackson forced the remaining Creek chiefs to sign a treaty in which the tribe ceded control over more than 21 million acres of territory to the United States.

 TEXT-DEPENDENT QUESTIONS

1. How many guns did the frigate USS *Constitution* carry?
2. How many British merchant ships did American privateers capture during the War of 1812? What was their value?
3. Where was the territory of the Creek tribe located?

 RESEARCH PROJECT

The British supported Native American tribes that waged war against Americans before and during the War of 1812. How did this warfare affect subsequent U.S. government policies toward Native Americans during the 19th century?

Chapter 5

Final Battles, and Peace

The defeat and abdication of Napoleon in the spring of 1814 freed British forces to expand their campaign against the United States. By summer, British veterans were arriving in North America to take part in a new offensive. The United States now faced the prospect of British invasion. In fact, British armies would attempt to invade the U.S. at three different points.

The British General George Prévost, who commanded all military forces in Canada, planned to invade New York. First, Prévost's men would gain control of

Mariland militiamen fight against an advancing British force at the Battle of North Point, near Baltimore. Victory in the European war enabled Britain to send large numbers of troops to America in the summer of 1814, but the U.S. military successfully resisted their invasions.

Lake Champlain, on the border between New York and Vermont. Many of the Vermont farmers, like others in the New England states, had opposed the War of 1812. They had even provided food and supplies to the British army. So Prévost decided that his 11,000-man army would advance along the western side of the lake, and attack the American garrison at Plattsburgh, New York.

The British Army captured the village of Plattsburgh on September 6, 1814, but the Americans withdrew, destroying bridges across the Saranac River as they retreated. British warships would need to gain control over the river so that the British army could cross safely.

Both the British and Americans had fleets of warships on Lake Champlain, and control of the waterway was not certain. The American naval fleet, commanded by Lieutenant Thomas Macdonough, included four large warships: USS *Saratoga* (26 guns), USS *Eagle* (20 guns), USS *Ticonderoga* (14 guns), and USS *Preble* (7 guns). The Americans also had ten smaller gunships. The British fleet was roughly equal in size, with four large warships and a dozen gunships. British commander Captain George Downie's flagship was HMS *Confiance*, the largest ship on Lake Champlain. The ship was capable of carrying 36 guns or more; however, *Confiance* was not quite finished, and so sailed into battle with only 16 usable guns.

On the morning of September 11, the British fleet approached the American ships, which had been anchored in a defensive position in Plattsburgh Bay. In a naval battle lasting more than two hours, the ships

 # WORDS TO UNDERSTAND IN THIS CHAPTER

bombardment—an intensive and sustained attack by bombs or artillery fire.

breastworks—a low, temporary defensive wall, often built from earth or logs to the height of a soldier's chest.

high seas—open waters of an ocean, beyond the limits of a nation's territorial waters.

This illustration from 1814 shows Macdonough's fleet defeating the British on Lake Champlain, September 1814.

of both sides were badly damaged. The *Saratoga* and *Confiance* had smashed each others' gundecks with repeated broadsides until both were nearly disabled; Macdonough then cut away an anchor that enabled the *Saratoga* to swing around so its undamaged guns on the other side of the ship could rake the *Confiance* with fire. Captain Downie was killed, and the British ships, unable to fire back, were forced to surrender.

Prévost had ordered a artillery barrage against the American defenses that morning, but once the naval attack failed there was no way his planned land attack could succeed. He called off the attack, and soon his men were retreating back to Canada.

Bombs Bursting in Air

A second invasion force came from Bermuda, where the British had a military base. Many of these soldiers were veterans of the Napoleonic Wars who had fought with the Duke of Wellington's army. They were led by General Robert Ross, and brought to North America on a fleet of warships commanded by Admiral Alexander Cochrane. They sailed for the Atlantic Coast, arriving at the Chesapeake Bay on August 19, 1814.

Secretary of War John Armstrong believed the British would attack Baltimore, but didn't think they would strike at Washington, D.C., the capitol. After all, Washington was a relatively small and unimportant town. Baltimore was larger and was home to many important businesses and industries. The capitol was therefore defended by a relatively small force, while more defenders were located at Baltimore.

The British, however, planned to attack both cities. On August 24, a British army routed the American defenders at Bladensburg. The Americans retreated in disorder, leaving the way open to Washington. Secretary Armstrong and other members of the U.S. government, including First Lady Dolley Madison, were forced to flee from the capitol, hastily packing vital papers so they would not be captured by the British.

When the British arrived, they set fire to the Capitol and the White House, in retaliation for the American burning of York the previous year. The flames were visible 40 miles away in Baltimore. Fortunately, a thunderstorm at dawn kept the fires from spreading. The British troops then returned to their ships and set out for Baltimore.

In the days following the attack on Washington, American forces prepared for an assault on Baltimore that they knew would come by both land and sea. The land assault began on the morning of September 12, when General Ross landed with an army of about 4,500 men at North Point, about 14 miles from Baltimore. About halfway there, Ross's army encoun-

This 1815 watercolor by George Munger shows the White House after it was set on fire by by British troops during the War of 1812. Although the fire gutted the rooms inside, the stone walls remained standing. The mansion was rebuilt after the war.

The British fleet stayed out of range of Fort McHenry's guns, so the defenders only fired a few shots at the enemy. One British sailor was wounded by American cannon fire, while four American soldiers were killed during the bombardment.

tered a force of 3,200 American militia under the command of General John Strickler. Although the British eventually forced the Americans to leave the battlefield, they suffered heavy casualties. Among the dead was General Ross. His successor in command, Colonel Arthur Brooke, allowed the American army to retreat to a strong defensive position in Baltimore.

To capture Baltimore, the British had to take Fort McHenry, which guarded the ocean approach to the city. Carefully, Cochrane maneuvered 16 of his fleet's smaller ships up the Patapsco River and placed them in two half-circles around the fort. At 7 A.M. on September 13, the ships began their **bombardment**. A large American flag flew over the fort as the attack continued for 25 hours. The British fired 1,500 bombshells at Fort McHenry. At first the cannons in the fort fired back, but their shots fell short. The British ships were anchored two miles offshore, out of range of the American artillery. There was nothing the defenders could do but wait for the shelling to stop.

During the night the British sent 1,000 additional troops to capture an American artillery post so that Brooke's men could storm the fort from the rear. However, this attack failed, and the overly cautious Brooke did not press an attack on the city.

On September 14, the British withdrew their remaining troops and sailed for the **high seas**. Without Fort McHenry, they could not take Baltimore. Cochrane sailed his fleet south to threaten another important American port, New Orleans.

An American attorney named Francis Scott Key watched the British bombardment of Fort McHenry from the deck of a British ship, where he was held captive. The September 1814 battle inspired Key to write a poem that he called "The Star-Spangled Banner." Soon after the British ships sailed out of Chesapeake Bay, printed copies of the poem began to appear on the streets of Baltimore. Singers set the verse to the tune of a popular drinking song, and over time, the song became America's national anthem.

Peace is Concluded

Discussions to end the War of 1812 began before the first shot had been fired and continued throughout the war. During the summer of 1814, a five-man delegation from the United States began peace negotiations with a team from Britain in the city of Ghent, Belgium. From London's point of view, the really important negotiations were taking place in Vienna, where the map of Europe was being re-drawn following Napoleon's defeat.

On December 24, 1814, a little more than three months after the British bombardment of Fort McHenry, American envoys signed the Treaty of Ghent to end the hostilities. The peace treaty essentially restored North America to the conditions that had existed before the war. The treaty did not mention either impressment or the Orders of Council, which had been named as causes of the war in Madison's message to Congress two years earlier. Now that Napoleon had been defeated, Britain had plenty of sailors and no need to board American ships in search of deserters, and the British government had revoked the Orders in Council even before the War of 1812 began.

On paper, the War of 1812 was over. But one final battle remained to be fought.

Battle of New Orleans

By mid-December 1814, Admiral Cochrane's fleet had arrived in the Gulf of Mexico. The British Army had been reinforced since leaving the Chesapeake Bay, and now numbered over 8,000 men. They also had a new commander: General Edward Pakenham, a tough veteran of the Napoleonic Wars. The British landed troops on the Louisiana coast, and began marching toward New Orleans.

After his victory over the Creeks, General Andrew Jackson had been placed in charge of the defense of New Orleans. His force included soldiers in the regular U.S. Army, as well as militia from Louisiana, Kentucky, and Tennessee. Civilian volunteers, including many African Americans, swelled his small force to about 4,600 men.

Jackson moved aggressively against the British, attacking their camp on December 24. He also ordered his men to set up ***breastworks*** to defend New Orleans. General Pakenham's men attacked the breastworks on December 28, but withdrew once the strength of the American defenses was clear. He waited for reinforcements, which arrived on January 1, 1815. A British assault launched that day appeared on the verge of success, but the British artillery ran out of ammunition and Pakenham called off the attack.

On January 8, 1815, Pakenham divided his force to assault the American defenses at New Orleans from two directions. Nothing went as planned, and the attack turned into a disaster for the British. More than 700 British soldiers were killed, including Pakenham, while 1,400 others were wounded and 500 captured. On the American side, casualties were practically nonexistent: six killed and seven wounded.

The British soon left the New Orleans area, planning to attack elsewhere. Before they could, however, news that the Treaty of Ghent had been signed reached both Admiral Cochrane and General Jackson.

American soldiers defend their breastworks during the Battle of New Orleans. The British general Edward Pakenham, with sword raised on the left, was killed during the fighting.

Neither side had known about the treaty, signed two weeks before the battle. The British fleet soon sailed back to the Bahamas.

News of the Battle of New Orleans gave many Americans the impression that Jackson's victory had forced the British to make peace. Thus this late victory convinced Americans they had won the war. And they had, in a way. Although the War of 1812 brought no major changes in territory or policy, it did bring a change in the relationship between Britain and the United States. Britain had been forced into a grudging respect for its former colonies and a greater appreciation of their economic importance for British industry. The young United States had ensured that it would remain independent of European rule. Also, with the threat of Native American attacks on the frontiers reduced, the U.S. could begin a process of westward expansion that would continue throughout the nineteenth century and end with a nation that stretched from sea to shining sea.

 TEXT-DEPENDENT QUESTIONS

1. What event during the spring of 1814 freed British forces to come to the United States and wage a military campaign?
2. Which general commanded the British soldiers that attacked Washington and Baltimore in September 1814?
3. What treaty ended the War of 1812? When was it signed?

 RESEARCH PROJECT

How does "The Star-Spangled Banner" unite Americans? Use the Internet to find out things that people have said about the national anthem, and write a report explaining why people still revere this song some 200 years after it was written.

Chronology

1793   The British government, while at war with France, asserts the "Rule of 1756," that says French ports that had not permitted American ships to land during peacetime could not open to American ships during the war.

1803   The Royal Navy begins to impress American seamen, forcing them to work on British ships.

1805   After capturing the American ship *Essex*, the British government rules that ships that travel between neutral and enemy ports can be seized as prizes of war.

1806   Napoleon issues the Berlin Decree, announcing a blockade against Great Britain and declaring that all ships engaging in commerce with Britain will be subject to seizure.

1807   In June, American warship *Chesapeake* is fired on by the British ship *Leopard* after refusing to be boarded. This creates an international incident. Later in the year President Thomas Jefferson tries to force the British to change their practices with the Embargo Act, but it results in economic disaster for merchants and is repealed in 1809.

1811   The Twelfth Congress takes office, with a large group of newly elected representatives known as the War Hawks. They begin to pressure President Madison to declare war. At the Battle of Tippecanoe, William Henry Harrison defeats Native Americans, leading Shawnee leader Tecumseh to support the British in North America.

1812   On June 18, the United States declares war on Great Britain. American attempts to invade Canada fail, resulting in the loss of Fort Mackinac, Fort Detroit, and Fort Dearborn. In August, the USS *Constitution* defeats the British frigate *Guerriere* in a battle off the coast of Canada. It is the first of many American naval victories during the war, and raises American morale. American privateers set out on the high seas, raiding British merchant shipping.

1813   After the Battle of Frenchtown in January, Native Americans massacre wounded American soldiers in the Raisin River Massacre. In April, U.S. forces capture and burn York (Toronto), the capital of Upper Canada. In September, American naval forces under Oliver Hazard Perry win the Battle of Lake Erie. At the Battle of the Thames on October 5, Tecumseh is killed and the British and their Native American allies routed.

1814   On March 27, Andrew Jackson defeats the Creek Indians at the Battle of Horseshoe Bend. On August 24, British troops burn Washington, D.C. In September, the U.S. wins a major victory over a larger British force at the Battle of Plattsburgh. On September 14, the British bombards Fort McHenry but their assault on Baltimore fails. On December 24, British and American diplomats sign the Treaty of Ghent. agree to return to the status quo from before the war.

1815   In January, Andrew Jackson wins a great victory at the Battle of New Orleans. The Treaty of Ghent is soon ratified and both sides cease hostilities.

Chapter Notes

p. 7   "paper bullets, bloody messages ..." quoted in Bradford Perkins, *Prologue to War: England and the United States, 1805-1812* (Berkeley: University of California Press, 1970), p. 399.

p. 9   "The War of Revolution ..." Benjamin Franklin, quoted in Dana Childress, *The War of 1812* (Minneapolis: Lerner, 2004), p. 5.

p. 10   "just and lawful" Transcript of the Northwest Ordinance (1787). http://www.ourdocuments.gov/doc.php?doc=8&page=transcript

p. 27   "the right to export our cotton, tobacco ..." Henry Clay, *The Speeches of Henry Clay,* vol. 1 (New York, A.S. Barnes, 1857), p. 40

p. 29   "a mere matter of marching" Thomas Jefferson, personal letter to William Duane, August 4, 1812. Preserved in the National Archives. http://founders.archives.gov/documents/Jefferson/03-05-02-0231

p. 31   "I come prepared for any contingency ..." William Hull, quoted in Nicole Eustace, *1812: War and the Passions of Patriotism* (Philadelphia: University of Pennsylvania Press, 2012), p. 48.

p. 35   "one of those uncommon geniuses ..." William Henry Harrison, *Messages and Letters of William Henry Harrison* (Indianapolis: Indiana Historical Society, 1922), p. 549.

p. 40   "Hurray! Her sides are made of iron!" quoted in A.J. Langguth, *Union 1812: The Americans Who Fought the Second War of Independence* (New York: Simon and Schuster, 2006), p. 206.

Further Reading

Benn, Carl. *The War of 1812*. London: Osprey Publishing, 2014.

Calloway, Colin C. *Shawnees and the War for America*. New York: Viking, 2007.

Childress, Diana. *The War of 1812*. Minneapolis: Lerner Publications, 2004.

Clarke, Gordon. *Major Battles of the War of 1812*. New York: Crabtree, 2012.

Daughan, George C. *1812: The Navy's War*. New York: Basic Books, 2013.

Ferry, Joseph. *The Star-Spangled Banner: Story of Our National Anthem*. Philadelphia: Mason Crest, 2015.

Languth, A. J. *Union 1812*. New York: Simon and Schuster, 2006.

Internet Resources

www.warof1812.ca

This Military Heritage website includes articles on many aspects of the war, a timeline, and reenactment information.

http://www.history.com/topics/war-of-1812

This History.com page on the War of 1812 includes biographies of key figures, as well as articles and facts about the war.

http://www.loc.gov/rr/program/bib/1812

The Library of Congress Guide to the War of 1812 includes links to manuscripts, broadsides, pictures, and government documents related to the war. It also provides links to external websites that deal with the War of 1812.

www.collectionscanada.ca/military

"From Colony to Country: A Reader's Guide to Canadian Military History" provides information about the War of 1812 from a Canadian perspective.

www.si.edu/Encyclopedia_SI/nmah/starflag.htm

Smithsonian website with facts on the Star-Spangled Banner and the War of 1812.

Index

Numbers in **bold italics** refer to captions.

SERIES GLOSSARY

blockade—an effort to cut off supplies, war material, or communications by a particular area, by force or the threat of force.

guerrilla warfare—a type of warfare in which a small group of combatants, such as armed civilians, use hit-and-run tactics to fight a larger and less mobile traditional army. The purpose is to weaken an enemy's strength through small skirmishes, rather than fighting pitched battles where the guerrillas would be at a disadvantage.

intelligence—the analysis of information collected from various sources in order to provide guidance and direction to military commanders.

logistics—the planning and execution of movements by military forces, and the supply of those forces.

salient—a pocket or bulge in a fortified line or battle line that projects into enemy territory.

siege—a military blockade of a city or fortress, with the intent of conquering it at a later stage.

tactics—the science and art of organizing a military force, and the techniques for using military units and their weapons to defeat an enemy in battle.